D0810611

ZORBA'S DAUGHTER

May Swenson
Poetry Award Series
Volume 14

ZORBA'S DAUGHTER

poems
by

Elisabeth Murawski

UTAH STATE UNIVERSITY PRESS
Logan, Utah
2010

Utah State University Press
Logan, Utah 84322-7800

© 2010 Elisabeth Murawski
foreword © 2010 Grace Schulman
All rights reserved

Publication credits appear in the acknowledgments.

Manufactured in the United States of America

Cover art "La Joueuse de Flûte" by Camille Claudel. Photo courtesy of Reine-Marie Paris.
Used by permission of Artists Rights Society.
Series cover design by Barbara Yale-Read

9780874217957 (cloth)
9780874217964 (pbk)
9780874217971 (ebook)

Library of Congress Cataloging-in-Publication Data

Murawski, Elisabeth
  Zorba's daughter : poems / by Elisabeth Murawski.
     p. cm. -- (May Swenson poetry award series ; v. 14)
  ISBN 978-0-87421-795-7 (cloth : alk. paper) -- ISBN 978-0-87421-796-4 (pbk. : alk.
paper) -- ISBN 978-0-87421-797-1 (e-book)
  I. Title.
  PS3563.U7228Z44 2010
  811'.54--dc22
                                     2010009601

For Alexia and Haley

CONTENTS

I heard music, anonymous and sublime, throughout my reading of the finalist manuscripts in this poetry contest. I wondered how to choose one of them when I wanted to award, or at least thank, a number of writers for letting me enjoy their vitality and skill. Then *Zorba's Daughter* leaped out at me with an urgency whose source was charged language. Time and again, I was compelled by the best word, the unpredictable phrase, the surprise.

The writer's name, I found out later, is Elisabeth Murawski, and I regret that the poems were unfamiliar to me although they have appeared in a chapbook and in journals. The voice is entirely new. It has a haunting, plaintive quality I find unforgettable, at times close to prayer. The poet transcends her subjects, presenting the details of personal experience in ways that become immediately recognizable to everyone: a Roman mass, a spelling bee, vandalism in an Elizabethan garden.

The author of *Zorba's Daughter* lives in a state of perpetual astonishment and dares us to enter her world. A visit to "Hatteras Lighthouse," which in other hands could be an ordinary seaside journey, is transformed here into a hair-raising adventure:

We laugh and pant for our hearts
pushed this far, each step harder
than the last, the air close and humid

so that our hair clings to our necks
and we gasp, forced to stop at landings
on this spiral to a man-made moon

Often the poems are startling for what they do not say. Murawski's silences are eloquent. She hints at universally painful themes: religious ambivalence, for one; incest for another. The sacred is her territory, but in writing of normative observances and codes of behavior she awakens powerful Catholic guilt and, by extension, our own culpability. Here is the memory of a mass in which the priest "speaks in Latin/or in Polish:"

I bow my head
to imitate the old man
who on Sundays stays for all the Masses,
locked in place
at the altar rail, face
buried in his hands,
hunched over and sad
as if, like me,
he'd done everything wrong.

Someone like him, I think,
could stop the nails
from going in.

Again in a delicate, almost casual, but poignant tone, she writes of loss in early childhood:

I watched the mouth death played
strange tricks about,

the lips a line pulled thin
as Mama's eyebrow. In every empty room
I faced her language in the dark.

There were too many vowels.
They stung like accidental tears.
They rolled like ice cubes off her tongue.

Murawski arrests our attention. She domesticates Bishop's keen observation, making small things large and commanding us to watch. Hearing mourning doves, she brings us to their song:

listen
they chorus. Here is
the underlying
sorrow of the world.

In the belly.
In the rock. In the black
holes of heaven.

Reading Murawski, I think of the poet for whom this series is named. I recall especially her wonder at the miraculous in the quotidian. Whether May Swenson's subjects are commonplace or unfamiliar, she presents them with an urgency that builds their impact. Murawski carries on that great tradition.

Grace Schulman

When everything goes wrong, what a joy to test your soul and see if it has endurance and courage! An invisible and all-powerful enemy—some call him God, others the Devil, seems to rush upon us to destroy us; but we are not destroyed.

I felt deep within me that the highest point a man can attain is not Knowledge, or Virtue, or Goodness, or Victory, but something even greater, more heroic and despairing: Sacred Awe!

Nikos Kazantzakis
Zorba the Greek

ZORBA'S DAUGHTER

ONE

ZORBA'S DAUGHTER

Night boasted it was eternity.
But here now
through the brown links of trees
the sun spills dawn.

Light's turn (dice on a table)
to be eternal, a current
to feed her house, abruptly
wake her like a thief. Who

will teach her divine
collaboration? Who will love
her dirty hands enough
to leave her head unshaved?

She goes barefoot as the sky,
nectarine slice on a spoon,
sweet coral carnation,
little fish

with wings in her heart,
tempted to fly
from the spear
she cannot escape, resolved

to die like Samson
braced against the pillars
of the temple,
roaring for his eyes.

ON ARRIVING AND DEPARTING

The moon is an ellipse
half-hidden by a silo.
Dry leaves rasp like paper.

I hold a microphone
close to the calf
in the cow's belly. Where is

the one pure thing?
A train whistle
wraps itself around

the wooden house, around
the calf's heartbeat.
Am I leaving the farm

or arriving? The red
of the barn in moonlight
turns gray

as the devil's face
when he sniped at Schubert
writing the four impromptus.

NORMAL: A SURGICAL LOVESONG

The lamp's
frayed cord. Wet
skin. The shock
enough to knock
the baby out and blow

a fuse. Where
did she go?
Was there a bear
or owl to guide?
An arrow

to annihilate?
The mother smears lard
on rye bread.
Sprinkles it
with sugar. The two

oldest siblings
sail records
a half inch thick
from the attic.
The father, drunk,

snores loudly
on the couch. King,
his vicious
German Shepherd, lies
pagan and alert

at his stocking feet.
The baby finds her thumb.
Her eyelids flutter.
She drifts
within reach.

SAFEWAY VIA DOLOROSA

The woman's hand
cranes over the lot,
drops, in possible
selection, lifts
again, momentarily

empty, put off
by blackening
leaves. Didn't Anne
Frank choke
on rotting lettuce?

How could a head of leaves
so rabbit-pelt
soft and light
possibly drop
at the same rate

as a rock?
She tears off a bag
to stuff
the lettuce in.
At the moment of choice,

a couple with a cart
nearly knocks her down.
The woman frowns
at the display,
something wicked

in the way the lettuces
are turned
on their sides,
the icy bed.
Children dying

in the fetal position.
She sneaks a leaf
into her mouth.
It tastes
like a hiding place.

THE INTERVIEW

I found her floating in the wishing pond,
all those pennies on the bottom
shining like stars.

They had to pry her from my arms.
Oh those hollyhocks, tall
and smug, I cried beside,

the mocking tiger lilies,
freckled as the Irish cop
who came to the house.

She was three.
She loved to feed the ducks
scattered crusts. That cop

kept pestering me
for the name of the town
with the wishing pond,

the name of the cemetery.
When I said I forget,
he smirked like a hollyhock.

Accused me of bearing
false witness, inventing
a sister for my sons.

Fickle ducks.
Crowding me now for bread.
I'm not the dead girl.

WINDY CITY

I consider alternatives
to never playing the piano,
to never making it
to the Louvre. I consider

black ribbons in my hair
for the downhill skier,
for the amaranthine village
overstocked with doves.

Before this very pool—
finding my voice, believing
in my knees,
the cushion on the floor,

in the song on the roof
and the windy noise of cars—
I am turning into leaves.
How deep is this pool?

Endless
as the mornings of the world.
What do I touch there?
A hand. A root system.

THE LIVING ROOM, MY SISTER WROTE, HAD
SEVEN WINDOWS

We are at risk, historians.
Who's to say
details we select

are soft enough, harsh
enough? How much do we
distort? My sister,

who counted windows,
could not remember
if I fell, if the hall

were yellow. Why
do some count windows,
others not? My graying

baby brother chews
the ice cube in his drink,
repeats himself:

we were not abused.
I want to pull his sagging
shoulders back

to breathe,
to save his heart. Silent,
I am yellow as the hall.

BEFORE THE AIR BECAME THE JOURNEY

It is Good Friday
and I am seven.
I don't understand the priest
who speaks in Latin
or in Polish,
but I like the hopeful smell
of candles burning.

Inching forward
on our knees,
we sway and shuffle towards
the giant crucifix
propped at the railing.
The men's heads are bare.
The women wear babushkas.
Everywhere I look
there are soles of shoes.

My turn. I stand
and stretch to reach
the bleeding instep.
An altar boy
wipes away my kiss
with a white handkerchief.

I bow my head
to imitate the old man
who on Sundays stays
for all the Masses,
locked in place
at the altar rail, face
buried in his hands,
hunched over and sad
as if, like me,
he'd done everything wrong.

Someone like him, I think,
could stop the nails
from going in.

HOME BURIAL SCENE

I faced the stony flesh my flesh
could not be here without
and did as I was told, kissed

her forehead, touched the spotted
hands lassoed by rosary beads.
Too young to prize the Poland

in her nose and chin, I stood
beside the metal box
she must be hiding in and listened to

the wax hiss down to glass.
I watched the mouth death played
strange tricks about,

the lips a line pulled thin
as Mama's eyebrow. In every empty room
I faced her language in the dark.

There were too many vowels.
They stung like accidental tears.
They rolled like ice cubes off her tongue.

WEDDING FALL-OUT

Ten, I wore a red hat
to the wedding, red
the color of weeping. Mine,

the bleak house, the torn
face-card. My sister flew
from our street like a stained-

glass butterfly. I wanted
her back, protection
from the king of the turning

doorknob. Hope had spots
on its skin like an old person's.
I climbed a ladder

made of sand and forgetting.
I lost the sky, decades
of clouds. The clay-

footed saints I turned to
cackled and shuffled, twirling
their blue umbrellas.

CHICAGO SPELLING BEE CHAMPIONSHIP

Only a handful of finalists
remained. My turn
to stand alone behind
the microphone,
pronounce, then spell,
pronounce again
my word. "Persuasion."

After "autocracy,"
which I'd never heard before,
after "mayonnaise,"
whose double "n"
must have registered
unwittingly
from the Hellmann's jar,
this was easy. "P-E-R"

I said, confident,
smug hare napping.
"S-V..."
and caught myself
in the turtle's dust,
the irretrievable
"v" flying out
over the footlights
into the darkened assembly hall
to sympathetic gasps
from the audience. No
second chances.

I stumbled out the rest
and stepped down.
If Ma reproached,
mercifully I've forgotten.
To the rock and sway
of Cicero Avenue's
dirty red streetcar,
I could hear my mistake

land again and again
in the same circle of hell
reserved for the misspelled,
the misbegotten.

Scant comfort now
to read the OED says "u"
is a differentiated
form of "v." That
Latin manuscripts
written in capitals
used only the V,

as in JVLIVS CAESAR.
Was I Calpurnia
in a previous life?
Dyslexic? For years

I berated myself
for that slip of the tongue.
Unable to forgive,
too ashamed
to admit it ever happened,
I kept turning one mistake
round and round
in my head
as if it were my life.

PUELLA

The spotted wine-
brown of her blood
stared back like
a sentence would

when she couldn't
read, its bird's-foot
tracks
on her girlish

underwear
breaking and
entering. Her
wooden tongue

clacked in her head.
A child was dying
in her shoes.
With her lips

she formed the word
"why,"
but the waves
outshouted her

as they always did,
caressing her
ankles, biting
her skin with salt.

THE MOON ACADEMY

You fly into the sky
wary as a rose
that's never bloomed this high.
The moon comes up
rich and full.

She asks you:
why are you lost
in the kingdom of the flying horse?
Why are the hats of your dolls
tilted and cross
with the bells of the Angelus?

I am tossed, you say,
like a child's rubber ball.
But the child is gone
before the ball comes down.
The child is stolen,
hidden in the deep woods.
(I have written in hatred
all over my mother's clothes.)

The sky darkens.
The moon disappears.
You come back to earth
but when you walk
it's with the heavy feet
of movie monsters.
The cradle scene of straw
continues to burn.

To hold your own
you must open to the moon's changes.
You must push off again
like a sea from the shore
leaving a trail of shells behind
for light to follow.

THE FISH

Wide as my body, half
as tall, the fish
lolled under
a rowboat tied to the pier,
its movements,
had the water been air,
like a fat Chinese kite's,
hovering.

In a movie, sinister
music might have played
finding such a fish—
groan
of cellos and basses.
But then there was only
the hot summer silence
of the afternoon
gripped at random
by a dog's distant barking.

The fish's belly was yellowed
by the sunlit water.
I couldn't see its head.

Distracted
by a divebombing dragonfly,
I turned
just for a second,
then looked back.
The fish was gone,
the brown-gold water empty
as the shrine of a god
no longer prayed to.

I decided not to tell.
Who'd believe me anyway—
a fish that huge
in muddy Lake Como!

My secret then,
to pull up through the years,
symbol of all I saw
and didn't want to see.

BLUE LADY

I shocked her when I said
I liked to study wars.

What I meant was
those orderly lists in the text
of causes and effects,

not bloodshed.
But I couldn't explain.

Anymore than I could say to her
blue was my favorite color
because of her eyes.

Blue is cold my mother said,
handing me her needle
to thread.

Grown, I would buy her dresses
in shades of cornflower,
royal, delphinium.

THE POTATO LOVERS

Of course, I hushed.
It's what they wanted.
My eyes were dry as powder.

Good dog, I buried
grief that night
in the funeral parlor.

Paternal hugs
stored in a trunk,
not yet tagged unseemly,

would be held against him
later, rotting cloth
of a suit no longer

a la mode. I'd mourn
in sleep, spend
a lifetime wondering

what it was I needed
to forgive. And draw
crooked trees afloat,

without roots, believing
in the strength of men,
hearing again and again

Mama's carping judgment
from the widow's throne:
I knew she'd crack.

PRIZE

She looks at me
through a caul of forgetfulness.
Does she want to be

understood? She who
could not watch
her own mother die

but locked herself in
the bathroom,
vomiting. I ask myself

why should I?
She was like
the morning glory's trumpet

in late afternoon,
disappointingly
folded in on itself,

hiding her heart
from view. I stroke
her hand, its skin

thin as a petal, knowing
she will never play
the music I hoped for.

FOR THE CAT ANTHONY

What better time to happen than the spring?
Who is my mother? Who is my father?
Our cat, part Manx, his tail
cut short by God, was killed by a car
in front of our house. Anthony
was three, never gelded, named by my son

without knowing what it meant to me, this son
so fond of animals, so in tune with spring
and innocence, I could not tell him Anthony
was a bad choice, the only name of my father—
boozer, short-fused trucker too poor for a car.
That he'd sit at table, tense as a lion's tail

batting air, and I'd wait for the tail
to suddenly stop, his fist flying out at one son
or another. I often dream of losing my car.
I have no happy memories of the spring.
Always lilacs turning brown and the breath of my father
stopped now, and no he was never an Anthony

to my mother, but a Tony, and no Anthony
either of Padua, greeting a guest, so the tale
goes, with the infant Jesus on his arm. My father
dead, the last night of the wake his eldest son
hushed my howl and it wasn't spring
but December and there was snow on the car.

I remember sitting quietly in the car
thinking blue horse thoughts of Anthony
who'd been so cruel and hard to love in spring
or any season. What stifled him like a stubby tail?
Our cat was buried in the garden while my son
said requiem prayers to his father

in heaven. I screamed the night my father
died, waking my aunts sleeping over. When the car
hit the cat, the driver apologized to my son
and all night I cried, I thought, for Anthony
to come back, to purr and stretch again, tail
a twitch of fur. I'm not prepared, ever, for spring.

So many years with a spring without my father,
I finally tell my son what's in a name, the tale
of Anthony not hit by a car.

DUSKY

This time I walk it off in the mall.
The slit of light, the eyes, the lip.
I study sandals under glass,

pearls harvested like fruit,
a veil white as salt.
The rats came out at night,

shapes rippling
like the coalman's belly
in the fun-house mirror.

His feral hand gripped mine
and I froze. O little girl,
I love you singing

to the pigeons and the peonies
overrun with ants.
Afraid of stairs,

the everlasting dark
stars fall from.
When he lifts you up, go limp

as a rabbit in the black pot
that held your sister
for the photo.

Think of the Monarch
skimming the pasture, landing
on the honey-colored cow.

ON FORGIVING THE GREAT PRICE

Hope in shreds, a medal torn
from a soldier's chest.
A book in the fire. Pearls

whisper in their shells
like the hush of rubber soles
in corridors. Who

will guide our hands to write
between the lines? The face
beneath the rubber mask

hides still another face.
A photo within a photograph.
Stacking Russian dolls. Heart

in a quiver, about to be fed
to the bow. Tree for a target
on some green mountain

where a reed plays in a wind
scattering sheet music. Wood
of the cross, the god in the box

set free. The blue and white
world slips out of reach
and the dark womb of the stars

enfolds us for its own,
a gown knitting itself
about the sins of the fathers.

FRIGHTENED BY ITALY

This prowling place of dark wine
and lilies has no ceiling,
leaves a trail of broken cameras.
Where is Francis and his bleeding
sun? The upside down Il Duce
swings and swings
a bitter incense. Titian
paints himself into yet another
crucifixion scene.
The little Goretti girl
who wore nothing special
to her murder, fell ripe
as a blood orange
to the molester's knife.
The earth shifts in place.
Rage rivers out
and preserves at the dinner table
all those family members
homely as grape leaves
stamping out life.

TWO

HATTERAS LIGHTHOUSE

We laugh and pant for our hearts
pushed this far, each step harder
than the last, the air close and humid

so that our hair clings to our necks
and we gasp, forced to stop at landings
on this spiral to a man-made moon.

Each window leaks a draft of cool,
reveals a scrap of blue tempting us up.
We pull back against the wall, stall

for earlier climbers who, descending,
barely touch an elbow or a sleeve,
brush past the life we hold. Kissed

by bracing chill at the final door
opening, we stare at the drop, the knots
of shrunken tourists on the beach.

The waves do their pre-historic two-step,
shuffle and glide, die and die
again, wind-tossed, noisy but solemn,

the moves classy as a model's
swinging her long legs down the runway,
reminiscent of that halt, moth

on a pin, to woo the audience,
before she pivots, charming
in reverse, then lopes backstage

into the darkness she came from,
tearing off her clothes in a frenzy
to meet the next "Allez!"

ARMS

Even your house knows
her arms want to surround you:
paintings slide to the floor.
The piano tries to hide
under the sofa.
The aluminum siding
turns blue. There are several

accidents. Scorned,
her arms grow long
and longer
until they reach across
two counties, patriotic
monuments, the tiger

in the Potomac.
The city darkens
with her need. But you
are not afraid.
Not even when you hear her
yellow fingers snapping
in the garden
to an old song, an old song,
an old song.

You who pity horses,
in their loneliness
born without arms,
lift the needle
and the mantra stops.
Her arms shrivel back
to where they came from.

Then all is quiet
in your own back yard.
You take off your shoes
and dance.
Your holy hair flies up.

ZONE

It's playing now, another
Bach suite for clavier.
Insistent as mourning doves.
Constant as the grief
for dead children.

What you held back
hurt what you gave,
these bits of amber
I cannot save
even if blessed

by the moon's light,
or running water.
Your smile blackens
like fired film
as it disappears

into the trees
beaded with spring.
Consider my need to destroy.
Consider these nails,
this hammer.

CAMILLE CLAUDEL AT LARGE

At least a foot of confetti
hides the floor. Streamers
whisper and gossip, an ocean

to walk through. So deep
a confession wrung from lipless
flutes. A city buried

with debris. I raise my hands,
charismatic looking back
to a mind clear and smooth

untroubled by spirits who would be
my clock to breathe by.
No one answers, pours champagne.

I pray in stone. Study
the maquette I would transform.
I could lead it under stars

small as eyeglass screws. Stars
do not judge or condemn.
Do not sit on my shoulder

like an unforgiving parrot
biting my ear. A red streamer
sticks to my shoe. A blue.

IN AN ELIZABETHAN GARDEN

Stone deities guard the fountain
in the sunken garden
with its table and benches,

beds of petunias purple
as Lent. Minerva
is whole. So are Jupiter

and Diana. But a vandal's
hammer has left Apollo
sexless as Abelard,

pouting Venus half scalped
and inconsolable.
Beyond the fountain,

a live oak leans parallel
to the lawn. Hints
of rainbow escape

from trunks of crepe myrtles.
Near the water, the gazebo
thatched with reeds,

the air swarms with gnats
restless as thought,
as the striped lizard

skittering on gravel,
obsessed with transport.
The magnolia's one

stunning blossom
calls *notice me,* insistent
as a mourning dove.

MOSQUE

Past sundown
you bring me here,
my first time inside
a mosque. Men
sitting cross-legged
on the floor
beside their teacher
briefly look up at us,
then turn back, on fire
to hear the word.

You ramble on
in praise of Muslim
art, exquisite
painted tiles, floral
carvings in teak,
your speech articulate
as a docent's, beauty·
your God. Abruptly

a young man kneeling
on the carpet
flings his body flat,
arms stretched out
to the divine
unseen. Not even ecstasy

stops you. I blush
for your blind spot,
my complicity.
Your handkerchief
keeps slipping from
my hair. We exit
through doors
whose workmanship
you extol. Lilacs
are dying in the garden.

I'm reminded
of a curious dream:
a white mosque in moonlight,
the dome luminous,
the cut-outs in stone
intriguing
as the labyrinth
in Chartres. I saw it
as if looking down
with a bird's eye, swirls
of sculpted openwork
inviting me in. A dream
I'll never tell you.

Tonight the wind
on the Potomac
is tearing up the moon's
reflection
as if it were a painful
photograph, scraps
of light riding
the dark water,
tossing and grieving.

MOURNING DOVES

They sound freshly wounded,
weeping their few
cracked notes. Lullaby

to the fly in the web,
the torn gazelle,
the Ice Man

with grass in his shoes
fighting sleep
on the glacier. Listen,

they chorus. Here is
the underlying
sorrow of the world.

In the belly.
In the rock. In the black
holes of heaven

and the sea. Leopardi,
drunk with melancholy,
would have loved

the North American
mourning doves
cooing

where their treasure is.
He'd have warmed
to their solemnity,

their blink and croon
charmed by the light
of dying stars.

THE TRAP

It's been years
since Beaton and *Vogue*—
her coming as a tree

to the Forest Ball,
upper body swathed
in leaves, face a mask

of black powder.
In her element
before the lens,

Chanel's oblivious
to the frame Avedon
puts her in:

posters plastered
on the walls behind
and overhead

like a blade:
Pourquoi HITLER.
To her left, Lady Liberty

stares beyond
the swirling slogan
of the barricades

at a far far better thing.
Avedon knows about
her handsome German

officer, the affair
postwar Paris can't
forget. Spared

the shaved head
of collaborators,
she was not led naked

through the streets.
A brief arrest
and then release to Swiss

exile. She welcomes
this respite
from quarantine, chooses

an outfit of jet, its collar
white as a nun's,
tucks a triple rope

of pearls under the belt.
In a hat
whose splash of brooch

suggests a cockade,
Chanel at 65
still exudes the style

she stole from England:
"elegant," she wrote,
"that is, detached."

The photo's not released
until she's dead.
By then, the irony

of woman, wall
and slogans juxtaposed
has lost its edge.

The young see
an aging celebrity
whose long thin neck

is turning sinewy,
her expression triste,
resigned, the white

gloved hand holding
a cigarette
going to ash

slightly lifted, extended
as if in benediction,
or to be kissed.

NOT TO BE

She watches the two of them
disengage,
observes the woman's eyes

following him
window after window,
out of range. She would like

to be loved like that,
passion of a hawk,
Una in the hand mirror,

the house built on rock.
He's off-limits to them both.
She suspects the woman,

doesn't trust herself,
wants to take from this moment
not his Irish

buck-toothed grin
but the way he shuts the gate
as if he cared too much.

LEDA IN THE PARK

Who's to blame
when Paris calls?
A crush on a swan!
A psyche in distress!
A kinky deity,
high on a livery
in the aquatic vein!

Could the couch
have cured her lust
for a swimming grace?
An acupuncturing?

Mother to a naval face,
could she have possibly
wrung his neck,
put him in his place,
sensing a destiny?

Tasting in his fleece
that fells,
a fragrance of ships,
a star that spells
an *Iliad*,
she could do no otherwise
than turn out her knees,
wrestle with a question mark.

ITALIAN EVENING

Perfect stand-ins for the Virgin,
they've escaped
their gilded frames,

in platform shoes and mini-skirts
ride mopeds, tresses
looped and pinned

from flying. This one,
with her prominent nose, sloe
eyes at a slant, Giotto's.

That one a twin
for Parmigianino's
Madonna of the Long Neck.

Imagine ancestors
sitting like stones for hours
while the masters prayed

with a burning brush, lit
candles with their eyes.
Imagine them returned to the world

and laying down their halos,
lush flesh eager
as grapes to be pressed.

ALMOST NAOMI

She loved me because I left you,
in her letters made me wonderful,
a praise too faint

in our couple days.
Had we married, she'd have hugged me
with indifference,

gray-blue eyes
glazed and wandering
till they fixed on a face-like

stain in the wallpaper.
In my heart I'd have known
she was holding someone

else, deemed perfect
with distance. Before
the letters stopped,

she wrote of tumors growing
back, radiation.
Did it ever subside,

her need for your life
not to change? Did she
accept your wife,

forget me as Ruth?
A pang at that last
thought, for I'm incurably

jealous. I imagine
her grave, in your hands
spikes of purple foxglove.

I LOSE MY WAY TO YOUR HOUSE

Nothing is ever
lost,
there are no mistakes
I keep telling myself

out loud, taking another
wrong turn,
and I am sweating
as if late for a curfew,

palms wet on the wheel,
feeling small
as a candle in a blackout
drawing fire

from Allied bombers
over Dresden, praying
for the light
to change, knowing

there will be no pianos
in your voice,
just a horse
of a different color.

OF A FEATHER

You bend forward
as you speak of China sky,
the moon torn from clouds.

Your dark eyes
do not follow me,
hold the warmth I want

hostage.
I who would fly beside you
like a crane

am the common shell
you will never pick up
on the beach.

I work the rim
of your indifference.
I'm just a woman

hiding stretch marks,
undressing
in the dark.

VIRUS

Predictable derby dance:
the catch, the toss,
the glide down your sleeve

to a glove. Between acts,
nausea, vertigo,
sighting the horizon

rebellious as the *Bounty*.
You preen
like a stainless steel

kettle full of steam
and about to whistle. Verbal,
your ill-mannered mouth

full of dead cow,
you test my skin's density
with tales of women

who threw their bodies
downhill like Jill.
I chew and chew

in desperation
the bread in front of me
hoping to restore the world

before this night,
but there's the scent of new leather,
and once again the present's

stolen by the past
with a flag's neat triangle,
the blast of taps.

MEDITATION, THE MORNING AFTER

I listen, still as quartz, to the mud of this earth.
I see a sacred image, a bouquet of white
nameless blossoms, edges turning brown, delicate

as old newsprint. This is discernment, my wooly
wish for happiness rubbed raw as a rope burn, carp
belly-up on the lake. An altered state dying to say

there are no mistakes, my life is perfect just
as it is, anchored to the barn. Old lovers'
backs and legs descend pure as sacramental wine.

Murders come out of the closet, all those empty coats.
A monarch springs up from the bouquet, child's soul
between worlds, the silence strict, fluid as silks.

UNREQUITED

My knowing all along
the formula
in black marble,

the golden house of God
not a pastorale.
The stage set: Keats

would drown, Teresa
pull out the dart
and throw it back,

catching the angel
off guard,
each candle burnt down

to a nub, hopeless
as my efforts to explain
the altar's sweet smoke

of indifference,
what I saw through,
what I could not believe.

THE PROPOSAL

What if I came to you
as one of your relics?
Clots of earth in my hair,
skin tinged green,

missing an arm.
You'd turn my chin
to peer into my eyes,
scrape my body clean.

I'd yield,
submissive as porcelain
fired for the last time.
Placed in a box

with a plastic lid,
at my feet
a small card printed
with my name,

the date of your find,
I'd be breathless
and white as wax
touched by ice.

If we listened hard enough,
we might hear
the whiplash of memory
sharpening between us.

TWO POETS: A SEQUEL

Long after the business of pain is closed
you write a poem about it,
this sharing of space in the same quarterlies
with a woman you loved once.
And I, seeing your poem as both complaint
and threat, am forced to ask
"Is it about us?" and you reply, "Who else?"

It might comfort you to know
that Nietzsche wrote
the poets lie too much.

Only now can I say
I hope you won't think it strange
that I've saved your letters,
what we used to call our eighteenth
century correspondence.
Or that I've bought a quilt like yours,
the Chinese red one with the tiny flowers,
only mine is white.
And that I've stopped drinking apricot brandy.

There's one special time I keep returning to.
Do you remember that afternoon
we drank water from the poet's spring?
Your mother
brought it all the way from Greece
to New York, just for you.
But you shared it with me.

We took turns sipping from the lip
of the tiny bottle,
waiting to see if it would work.

The water, I mean.
Our deep image.

GROOMING

Come to the mirror.
Break in. Learn
the other side.

Behind the face
crests a wave
darker than war.
Marry it.

The wave gives back
what you get.

Resist
the undertow
and tangle,
shimmering
with the body.

Break out. Shun
sorting.
Confirm what *is*

by experience
only. Take an ax
to the moon
on the lake.

Watch it
circle back.

Dry your hands.

THREE

METAPHYSICAL

For years now
I've turned to you in doubt,
like a charismatic

opening the Bible,
my finger drawn
to the exact word

where you'd speak to me
in confirmation,
or warning. Forgive me.

I haven't always
listened
when I've asked you, John Donne,

to undo the dark. Anoint
my forehead. Guide
my hand beyond pages

that you've left
to be my light. Bless
my squinting third eye.

LONG AFTER DARK AT THE CHURCH CARNIVAL

I have an itching palm to situate the stars,
to chart the cost and progress of a soul.

Maybe this is how a widow wants to feel
breaking the token clot of earth between
her fingertips. As if the power had left it.

The beach scene came right because we were
expectant, still full of hopes.

I am a child again, unable to explain
the hole I am digging. Who moans?

We bring to each other the same degree
of trust we bring to ourselves.
The hartebeest's horns are shaped like a lyre.

Do not tell me though I ask you
where strawberries grow on the side of a cliff.

Long after dark at the church carnival
I am praying, predictable as cat's-cradle.
I keep looking up the moon's sleeve.

There is a sharp lull into new feeling
being thrown back again into the sea.

ON HEARING A LECTURE ON STARS

There are too many of them.
They shrink the earth
to a town. I am turned

into an ant
on the sidewalk, afraid
of a shoe. They destroy

my God, too. Who
is left to hear, to count
every hair,

every sparrow?
The houselights flood.
Outside, the sun's

a hollow hand
conning my skin
back to life. I scan

the sky, no stars
in sight. Door to door
I carry old wines

in a suitcase,
my window on Sinai
smashed by an astronomer.

THE CHAPEL THAT TEMPTED O'KEEFFE TO
BECOME A CATHOLIC

A white linen throw, homely
as a blank canvas,
tops the square altar stone

large enough to pin down
Isaac. Did the artist rejoice
in the weave? Did the woman

recall the child she lived
without? Two wrought iron
candle-holders

curve like horns of doubt
on the lectern made of driftwood.
Raindrops like fingertips

tap in code. No hiding here
from the wilderness.
Christ dies again

in a sky-blue loin cloth.
Unstained, the windows weep
and blur the red hills.

AT THE SMALLEST NATIONAL CEMETERY, BALLS BLUFF, VA

The sun pales,
all of its blood let.

The air is thick with devil's
darning needles. Tops

of trees whisper
victory / surrender....

We can almost hear
sharp cracks of rifles,

human animal cries,
the whinnies of drowning horses.

PLANES

An hour ago, alive
but losing power,
the large moth kept bumping

into furniture,
tables and chairs
like mountains in fog

a pilot must cross without
instruments. I thought
it flew outdoors

but here it lies, grounded
on the shag beside
a toy purple plane

with yellow wings.
If Tai were here,
he'd poke the skin

as I do now, verify
nothing works. Mouthing
a buzzing sound, he'd "fly"

his purple plane
to make-believe towns
where no one dies.

Far away, then closer,
a noise like thunder.
Passing jet.

I lift the moth
and think of silk,
the weight of Bible paper.

KEY OF HEAVEN

Its clasp is broken,
covers frayed, pages missing
or loose, warm gold of edges

tarnished, dishwater gray.
I remember her praying
with glass rosary beads

the color of honey or beer,
never with this book. When
she carried it to her first

communion, she was fifteen,
old enough to pin up her hair,
America still a bystander

at the Great War. A child
has scrawled in pencil
on the flyleaf where my mother

wrote the year *First mass was held
in Robinson.* John tells me
how he found it, clearing out,

how he'd opened at random
to the verse: *Let not
your heart be troubled,*

nor let it be afraid.
And he finds the words again,
for me, though he's the one

facing surgery, the ticking
aneurysm. For days
we've tiptoed around death

as if it were a colicky baby
fast asleep. *Take it* he says,
brooking no refusals,

the way our mother would.
I cradle the *Key of Heaven*
as if it were a wounded bird, say

but it means so much to you,
knowing it comforts him
to give up what he thinks I want.

ALL THE THINGS I COULDN'T SAY

It was the hour
of creeping school buses,
nearly three

when your car soared
from the overpass,
broke Angel's back

and snapped your neck.
All for a rush
at double the speed limit.

You could't feel
the flames edge up
to your waist. Did you need

a war, a hero's place
at table? You'd always
wished to fly. See

how your friends in their grief
love one another.
How your brother's knees

beside the coffin
seem glued to the rug.
Do you think you deserve

such devotion? You did.
You do. I stamp my foot
at your bravado.

Death, that cheap mourner,
has come to the wake
as a red car. It rolls

over on its back,
wheels turning to a music
only you can hear.

CRECHE

East of the star,
spiked snowflake on fir,
a cloth dove, pinned

to a twig, flies shotgun
above the scene. The magi
are still en route;

only shepherds lean
on the periphery, bursting
with stories of strange

music, a stranger birth.
Drawn like a magnet
to this ersatz stable,

a small boy kneels,
parka unzipped, stubby
fingers itching

to rearrange the figures
as he would his toys:
shove the shepherds in

closer so they can see
the baby; the donkey's
lonely outside. The boy

won't touch a thing,
someday may learn
how St. Francis in his joy

started this custom
with live farm animals,
told the people of Greccio

to light up the sky
with torches (for the star).
That first creche, unlike

this one, smelled of dust
and dung, perfume
to the saint's nostrils

as he sang the gospel,
the infant borrowed for a day
slippery in his arms.

SCULPTURE: *THE YOUNG ACROBAT*

From a rolled up sleeve, one strong arm
thrusts the baby high with a force
not unlike a birth, the push away

from home, familiar seas. Aloft,
the infant leans forward on air, as if
to ask *why am I here, the ground's*

a long way down. Naked, he lies there,
his sex masked by a patch of cloth, pawn
of a hand's skill, nimble toes

curled under. His tiny fingers
separate, the index of the left hand
and the little finger of the right

slightly raised as if about to grasp
what appears beyond his reach, his mother
perhaps, who may also be an artist

of the ring: leaping on and off
a horse's back, somersaulting to a waltz,
twirling by her hair or her teeth.

Helpless to wend his way to her arms,
he must bear the thrill of heights, the smell
of fear, the seed of wanting more

than feeling safe, this danger his
to claim, balanced in a father's hand, eyes
on hold, learning to be perfectly still.

SMALL FIRES—NAGASAKI

The wind when it comes
is warm. There is no home
that isn't leveled

or burning. She barely
feels the tug
on her nipple, or sees

the blue-white dribble
on her baby's chin,
his swollen belly,

the one tree
left standing, its trunk
and branches a Y

incision, its few leaves
whispering
like witches. Leaning

by itself on the sky,
the gate of the temple
resembles pi,

an irrational number.
Small fires flicker. Empty,
she lets him suckle,

the child in her arms
who may die
or live without her.

LULLABY OF THE TRAIN

With eyes like empty
begging bowls
the orphan gypsy girls

have stopped complaining
of shoes that pinch
their toes, of dresses

with holes. The town
clock releases
a knight on horseback,

announces the hour.
The children can't tell
time yet. Numbers

on paper, they shuffle
forward, too weary
and hungry to cry

or look back.
The German nun waves
to her charges, obedient

as shadows. *Click clack*
go the wheels
kissing the railroad track,

lullaby of the train.
Click clack, click clack
to the smoky town in Poland.

ONE EYE

The children do exactly as they're told.
They stand in line. *Let's play a game.*

First or last, it doesn't matter.
There will be no prize.

The economy of lead: to make the most
dead. How many can he pierce

with one bullet? He fires
when the row is ruler straight. All

fall but one, whom he beheads.
Next time, he'll pack them tight

as fish. The dominoes lie flat
and still. He wipes the blade

of his bayonet. Their eyes pursue him
like a dog, street after street.

CHILD IN ART THERAPY

She draws a house
without doors or windows.
A tree rises higher

than the roof. Smoke
from the chimney
heads for the sun

half cut off
by the paper's edge.
No people stand or walk

on the grass. Asked
why, she says
they're bad

and locked indoors.
Suggestible,
she draws a single window

and a head with curls
looking out,
one pearl

of a teardrop
under each eye,
a turned down mouth.

THIS WAY, THAT WAY

My clothes tap and whisper
at the dryer window,
fall back into darkness

and heat, on the brink of rising
again. Like me
missing a mother's arms,

they go in circles,
kiss the window good-by,
hello. When the cycle

stops, I'll sort and fold.
I'll hug everything,
even those towels thrown in

to balance the load,
as if they were warm
imperfect children.

AT RISK

There it was, a longing
I swear I'd lost.

I wept as if in exile,
holding to my cheek

the sea-green turquoise ring
from the pueblo (a pattern

in the stone like clouds). Was I still
under the mountain's spell

if all I could hear was its call
to a wildflower peace?

Must I return to it, like Cezanne
drawn to the silhouette

of Sainte-Victoire? At Mass today,
the kiss of peace,

I embraced a man whose wife
is dying of cancer. Shameless,

I enjoyed his thirst,
before I pulled back. Tonight,

I'm a woman lying on a couch
lit by a hundred watt bulb,

lulled by the running
of the dishwasher. Hardly

an odalisque. I look around me
at a roomful of paintings

and books, what I have left
to protect. I could say

the mountain is *here*.
Why isn't that enough?

I could ask the dying wife.
She would pity my thirst.

PRETENDING IN THE SHOWER TO BE BLIND

I rinse and rinse
in this voluntary dark
wishing I cared enough

for those beggars at the gates
in another Alexandria
gate of the sun

gate of the moon
to give them
what is dear to me:

the Chinese gilt figurine
the olivewood madonna
Kuan Yin in alabaster

shoulders and neck
perfectly bent
back to the world

all these little things
acquired
for simple beauty's sake

in my mind
I try to hand them over
but it's impossible

I open my eyes
my skin is clean
water drips like tears

from the shower head
I twist the faucets
hard and shiny as coins

PATIENT

Your letter arrives
with a second envelope inside,
wrapped in a sheet of paper.
Each end's fastened
with a safety pin, a paper
diaper, on both sides of which
you've penned *Be careful*
in heavy ballpoint.

I am lucid, you write,
citing for the first time
the name of your shrink,
and include a poem about
a lady with a stick
called "You're Wrong, Sam.
It's Done Enormous Harm."
Beneath the poem you've scrawled
I may live.

You don't explain when I phone.
I imagine you dragging
your pocket comb
through a mass of tangled hair.
Your voice careens
up and down the scale
too fast to stop
and you laugh
as if I'm supposed to *know*.

The following week I hear
you've been admitted
to the psych ward, signed
yourself in. Who exists
under the mask you've ripped away?
I decide not to visit you there.

I think of rows of plastic babies
in Kresge's Five and Dime
when we were kids. Barely
three inches long, wrapped
in thin cotton blankets, pink
or blue, fastened
with small gold pins.

We held them close,
although nothing on their bodies moved,
and their painted eyes stared up
as if there were things in this world
they didn't want to see.

YAK

Led to a bridge
that fails to hold,
down I go,

never to know
your hand
again. Falling,

my horn's
a letter in air,
a turning

prayer wheel.
Tell me, master,
of trees

I've never seen,
of what the wind does
to leaves

and everything
born. The sun bathes
the snow, and you

cannot help.
I feel the cold
splash

of the blue lake.
Your sacks of salt
drag me under.

AFTER THE FLOWER

And where shall we go?
Ask the submerged things.
> Pablo Neruda

Neruda molts in his diving suit.
The hose and shoes erode,
the metal sheath waves in slow

motion, lily on a stem.
Called to the supper that lasts,
he has lost all boundaries,

speaks to the dead, to the rose
on pilgrimage, his words like doves
set free from a flood.

It is communion at its most extreme,
the total loss of what was thought
to be essential, a kingdom

of equals at table
destined to become and become.
Submerged things fall apart,

yield to the weight of water,
an emerald city. Neruda hobnobs
with the ribs of a whale,

swims into curves of calcium
spouting song like a troubadour
sworn to lady earth.

VANISHING POINT(S)

In the two days
since I've heard,
I've seen Jane in line
at Loew's, buying melons
in Safeway, rising up
in the Library of Congress

to applaud a performance
by the Leipzig Quartet.
The likeness can be strong
or faint, just enough
for a double take, a jolt
to fan guilt. Mendelssohn

survived his sister Fanny
by less than a year, sought
her presence in each note
of the F Minor quartet.
One might argue
Felix wore himself out

saying good-by. Did he see
her everywhere? White hair,
narrow shoulders...that woman
in tweed taking communion,
so like Jane! How many times
must the dead die?

GLASS

Escape wraps her like a symphony half to come.
She can only imagine the smell of April.
Here are yellow bricks left over
from a war that ended too soon. And fresh
green grass too far away to tell.

To reassure she speaks her name aloud.
Petals and stems drop their rainbows
on the floor, walk her body into daylight,
into the terrors of her skin blossoming.
She moves through doors where babies are safe

and priests reveal murders of the soul
to protect the innocent. There are no exits
for desire. The blue heron folds its legs
and flies over. The gaunt freedom
in its wings' slow dance affirms

like a chill. No deliverance in sight.
She investigates the chapel
for a hint of an explanation. The sun
blazing through an art deco window
colors the host lifted up a Chinese red.

THOUGHTS ON ST. AGATHA

For Marcy

Target of a Roman consul's
lust, she would not
submit, not even when
the rack stretched her taut
as a sailor's knot.

Faith intact, virgin
foolish for her God, she could
only look to heaven
(Tiepolo would capture it,
that lifting up of eyes)

when the blade sliced
through each breast. Legend has it
Peter sent an angel
to restore the severed flesh,
a miracle that galled

her pagan hosts. Enraged,
they rolled her naked body
over heated stones,
then tossed her back to die,
unwanted catch, on a litter.

She is invoked for cure
of cysts, suspicious
lumps, papillomas. Early
paintings of the saint
show a plate, two mounds

the faithful took for loaves.
Thus began the church's custom
of blessing bread
on Agatha's feast. Priestess
of laughter, Marcy

would see the humor
in this mistaking what a bra
holds up for bread.
She too faced zealots
with knives. Dealt

a double blow, mastectomies,
she joked after surgery
"I'm flat as a flapper!"
Ordered chicken *breast*
on the first anniversary.

Those mornings she'd like
to wake up whole,
Marcy hugs both children
to her chest
like an amputee who swears

the sawed off limb exists.
It was here and here
they nursed, her rack
not only the stab of absent
flesh but also fear

she'll be dismissed
before their lives
unfold. No Agatha
with eyes raised skyward
to a better world,

Marcy focuses
on this one, on Jacob's
stubby fingers
guiding a yellow crayon
to make a sun.

On Rachel's perfect feet
skimming the carpet
in a dance
optimistic as a wine glass
raised "Lechayim!"

EARTH DAY

After the warning dream,
you put your life in order,
arrange to give away the dog,
your only mourner,

buy the cemetery plot.
Your skin is soft, the years
kind. You're ready for anything
but this death, who arrives

looking sexy and cool
as the cellist
on the upper west side
you loved for his indifference.

Your eyes meet over wine,
dark as a dying father's blood.
Younger with each step,
you invite him up, turn back

the sheets of silk. Starker
plays Bach on the stereo,
the Suite in G for cello,
unaccompanied.

NOTE FROM A TRAIN

So it doesn't matter then,
this slow delivery, if I am
to love, to follow my heart.

In the eyes of the world,
I play the fool, obedient
to the hilt. I dance with hurt

to bring no further hurt.
I kneel and stretch out my arms:
Mary in Elizabeth's court.

Forgive me. I am slightly drunk.
This is what I want:
to celebrate the sun at work

behind every beheading.
To bow to its corollary,
pulling into the station.

ON THE HIGH SPEED TRAIN TO VENDOME, I SEE A WOMAN WHO LOOKS LIKE MADAME CEZANNE

I try not to stare.
She leans back and closes her eyes,
brows plucked, no lipstick,
bare throat and lobes

jewels enough. The train starts,
will glide from Paris to Vendome
in less than an hour, silken
and smooth as a limo. I think

of Chopin frail in coaches.
To Sand in Nohant and back again,
the jolting murderous.
Would he trade centuries?

Meanwhile, my lady sleeps,
and I am struck again
by the resemblance
to Hortense, her hands clasped

neatly in her lap
as Madame posed for Paul
in the conservatory. Fields
of yellow rape stream by,

the horizon jagged
with steeples. Near Vendome,
she jerks awake, rises
to expose the full streak

of leopard-print sweat suit.
Balancing in the aisle,
she's a cypress blown in Aix,
covered from neck to ankle

with splotches of black and gold,
her priceless leopard self
unfinished
but perfectly realized.

PHRYGIAN

My father, kissing me,
raised my atomic weight.
Strike my skin and it rings
like a gong.

Spared his touch,
a dozen yellow roses
spread like hair,
mine on a pillow

before my body froze
in this posture
colder than ice—
his glittering destruction.

My lips make no sign.
To restore my voice,
he must take the river
for his house

and bathe his fault
until Pactolus's sands
in shimmering exchange
turn golden.

ACKNOWLEDGMENTS

Alembic	Chicago Spelling Bee Championship
The American Voice	Safeway Via Dolorosa
Apalachee Review	On Arriving and Departing
Artemis	The Moon Academy
Birmingham Poetry Review	Grooming
Chautauqua Literary Review	Unrequited
Chelsea	Long After Dark at the Church Carnival; On Forgiving the Great Price; I Lose my Way to Your House; Zorba's Daughter
Connecticut Poetry Review	Home Burial Scene
Crab Creek Review	Windy City
Crazyhorse	For the Cat Anthony
Cumberland Poetry Review	Key of Heaven
Cutbank	Yak
Descant	Meditation, the Morning After
The Dubliner	Lullaby of the Train
88: A Journal of Contemporary American Poetry	Glass; Arms; Wedding Fall-out; The Proposal; After the Flower
Elixir	Zone; Earth Day; At the Smallest National Cemetery, Balls Bluff, VA
FIELD: Contemporary Poetry and Poetics	Puella; Phrygian; On the High Speed Train to Vendome, I See a Woman Who Looks Like Madame Cezanne
Fine Madness	Not to Be
Fulcrum	Sculpture: The Young Acrobat
Gargoyle	The Chapel that Tempted O'Keeffe to Become a Catholic
Illuminations	Blue Lady; Prize
Image	Mosque; Mourning Doves
The Literary Review	Camille Claudel at Large
Many Mountains Moving	Normal: A Surgical Lovesong; Of a Feather
Margie	All the Things I Couldn't Say; One Eye
Meridian	Leda in the Park; Patient
Midwest Quarterly	In an Elizabethan Garden

Natural Bridge	Almost Naomi
New Republic	The Potato Lovers
Ontario Review	Creche; Italian Evening
Poet Lore	Note from a Train
Poetry Daily	Hatteras Lighthouse
Puerto Del Sol	On Hearing a Lecture on Stars
Pulpsmith	The Fish
Quarterly West	The Living Room, My Sister Wrote, Had Seven Windows
South Dakota Review	Dusky; At Risk
Tar River Poetry	Two Poets: A Sequel; Planes; Vanishing Point(s)
32 Poems	This Way, That Way
Tiferet	Metaphysical
Tough Times Companion	Child in Art Therapy
Verse Daily	Zorba's Daughter
Virginia Quarterly Review	Hatteras Lighthouse; The Trap
Willow Springs	Pretending in the Shower to be Blind; Before the Air Became the Journey
The Yale Review	The Interview; Virus

"Frightened by Italy" © 2005 by The Antioch Review, Inc. First appeared in *The Antioch Review*, Volume 63, No. 4. Reprinted by permission of the editors.

"Thoughts on St. Agatha" won third prize in the 2000 Ann Stanford Poetry Prize contest. It originally appeared in *Southern California Anthology*, now the *Southern California Review*.

"The Fish," "Meditation, the Morning After," and "The Moon Academy" also appeared in the chapbook *Troubled by an Angel* (Cleveland State University Poetry Center, 1997).

I am deeply grateful to Grace Schulman and Michael Spooner for giving *Zorba's Daughter* a chance to fly and to say "Here I am." A special note of thanks to Walter Cummins for his support, advice, and friendship, and to Jane Frakes, a beacon of strength and hope, for her faith and love. Finally, a toast to Frederick Chopin, whose 200th birthday we celebrate this year. His music has truly enriched my life.

Elisabeth Murawski is the author of *Moon and Mercury (Washington Writers' Publishing House)* and two chapbooks, *Troubled by an Angel* (Cleveland State University Poetry Center) and *Out-patients* (Serving House Books). Over 200 poems have appeared in journals that include: *The Yale Review, The New Republic, The Virginia Quarterly Review, Field, Ontario Review, Antioch Review, The Southern Review, The Dubliner, Poetry Northwest,* and others. "Abu Ghraib Suggests the Isenheim Altarpiece" won the 2006 Ann Stanford Prize (USC). The present volume has been a finalist for the Field Poetry Prize, the Brittingham and Pollak Poetry Prize, the Blue Lynx Prize for Poetry, and The Journal/OSU Poetry Prize.

Born and raised in Chicago, she moved to Washington, DC in 1960 and recently retired from the U.S. Census Bureau where she worked as a training specialist. She holds an MFA from George Mason University. She has been awarded residencies by The Helene Wurlitzer Foundation, the Vermont Studio Center, and the Achill Heinrich Boll Association. In 2008 she was a Hawthornden fellow. She currently lives in Alexandria, VA.

THE MAY SWENSON POETRY AWARD

This annual competition, named for May Swenson, honors her as one of America's most provocative and vital writers. In John Hollander's words, she was "one of our few unquestionably major poets." During her long career, May was loved and praised by writers from virtually every major school of American poetry. She left a legacy of nearly 50 years of writing when she died in 1989. She is buried in Logan, Utah, her birth place and hometown.

Main

PORTLAND PUBLIC LIBRARY SYSTEM
5 MONUMENT SQUARE
PORTLAND, ME 04101

WITHDRAWN